FEELINGS

HAPPY

by Alissa Thielges

# dance

# hug

Look for these words and pictures as you read.

# grin

# laugh

# laugh

Maddie is happy.
She laughs at a joke.

dance

Joey feels excited.
He dances around.
He is happy.

## grin

Hannah is happy.
She loves to bike.
She grins as she rides.

## hug

Carl is very happy.
His friend is here.
They hug.

Happy people often feel thankful.
They say kind words.
Then others feel happy, too.

Sharing helps others feel happy. What makes you happy?

## dance   hug

Did you find?

## grin   laugh

Spot is published by Amicus Learning, an imprint of Amicus
P.O. Box 227, Mankato, MN 56002
www.amicuspublishing.us

Copyright © 2025 Amicus.
International copyright reserved in all countries.
No part of this book may be reproduced in any form without written permission from the publisher.

Library of Congress Cataloging-in-Publication Data
Names: Thielges, Alissa, 1995–author.
Title: Happy / by Alissa Thielges.
Description: Mankato, MN : Amicus Learning, [2025] | Series: Spot feelings | Audience: Ages 4–7 | Audience: Grades K–1 | Summary: "What makes kids feel happy? Encourage social-emotional learning with this beginning reader that introduces vocabulary for discussing feelings of happiness with an engaging search-and-find feature"— Provided by publisher.
Identifiers: LCCN 2024017541 (print) | LCCN 2024017542 (ebook) | ISBN 9798892000802 (library binding) | ISBN 9798892001380 (paperback) | ISBN 9798892001960 (ebook)
Subjects: LCSH: Happiness in children—Juvenile literature. | Happiness—Juvenile literature.
Classification: LCC BF723.J4 B33 2025 (print) | LCC BF723.J4 (ebook) | DDC 152.4/8—dc23/eng/20240502
Classification: LCC BF723.H37 T44 2025 (print) | LCC BF723.H37 (ebook) | DDC 155.4/1242—dc23/eng/20240508
LC record available at https://lccn.loc.gov/2024017541
LC ebook record available at https://lccn.loc.gov/2024017542

Printed in China

Ana Brauer, editor
Deb Miner, series designer
Kim Pfeffer, book designer and photo researcher

Photos by Getty Images/1shot Production, 1, Imgorthand, 8–9, kali9, 12–13; Shutterstock/mimagephotography, cover, PeopleImages.com - Yuri A, 10–11, Pixel-Shot, 6–7, Q88, 3, WBMUL, 14; Stocksy/Santi Nuñez, 4–5